ETHNIC IDENTITY

BRINGING YOUR FULL SELF TO GOD

STEVE TAMAYO

8 STUDIES
FOR INDIVIDUALS
OR GROUPS

Life
Builder
Study

INTER-VARSITY PRESS
36 Causton Street, London SW1P 4ST, England
Email: ivp@ivpbooks.com
Website: www.ivpbooks.com

While any stories in this book are true, some names and identifying
information may have been changed to protect the privacy of individuals.

Originally published in the United States of America in the LifeGuide® Bible Studies
series in 2021 by InterVarsity Press, Downers Grove, Illinois
This edition published in Great Britain by Inter-Varsity Press 2021

British Library Cataloguing-in-Publication Data
A catalogue record for this book is available from the British Library.

ISBN: 978-1-78974-330-2
eBook ISBN: 978-1-78974-348-7

Printed in Great Britain by Ashford Colour Press Ltd, Gosport, Hampshire

Inter-Varsity Press publishes Christian books that are true to the Bible and that
communicate the gospel, develop discipleship and strengthen the church for its
mission in the world.

IVP originated within the Inter-Varsity Fellowship, now the Universities and
Colleges Christian Fellowship, a student movement connecting Christian Unions in
universities and colleges throughout Great Britain, and a member movement of the
International Fellowship of Evangelical Students. Website: www.uccf.org.uk. That
historic association is maintained, and all senior IVP staff and committee members
subscribe to the UCCF Basis of Faith.

CONTENTS

GETTING THE
MOST OUT OF
ETHNIC IDENTITY

E thnicity shows up on every page of the Bible.
Discovering that God has a great deal to say about ethnicity might come as a shock. We expect the Bible to tell us about Jesus and how to live, but perhaps we don't expect to see our ethnicities affirmed or challenged.

Hearing the Bible on ethnicity makes the Scriptures feel freshly relevant. We may receive confidence to explore our own identities. If ethnicity is a gift from God, it may change the way we interact with family, friends, and enemies.

Engaging this material can lead us to speak out with our small voices against systemic injustices. Because ethnic tensions jump out to us in Scripture, we won't be surprised when they appear in real life. And we'll have hope for reconciliation.

WHY CARE ABOUT ETHNICITY?

This study may be difficult. Your family tree may hold villains and victims. Maybe you've been ashamed of a particular ethnic community to which you belong. This conversation has the potential to be challenging. But it's worth it.

Our world is growing more diverse with every passing year. Broad categories work less well, leaving us more aware that people have different ethnic histories from our own. Injustices, disparities, and tragedies fill our newsfeeds and occupy troubled corners in our minds.

We no longer have an option to ignore our ethnic identities. What a blessing, then, that God is not silent. Through the Bible, God shapes our engagement with ethnicity. He speaks into our lives, our relationships, and all we do. Will we listen?

RACE, CULTURE, AND ETHNICITY

Race is one way of categorizing the world. Talking about race uses the language of biology: skin color, physical features, hair, blood. We try to use these characteristics to create categories: White, Black, Asian, Native.

Arbitrary social constructions of racial categories allow a dominant group to hold sway over others. Racialized power hierarchies were initially justified based on perceived racial differences. Over time, these hierarchies became systematized and now operate by default. Racism evolves. Race is a powerful illusion.

Culture is another way of fitting people into categories. When we talk about culture we're talking about the artifacts and practices of particular groups of people: food, clothing, music, holidays, customs, language, and so on. Culture operates at many levels. Countries have cultures. Cities have cultures. Even families have cultures.

At some levels, cultures can be easy to cross and learn. I can learn to eat your food. You can speak my language. We can go to another cultural neighborhood and drive on their highways and wear clothing typical to people in that place. In fact, learning culture is one way we express love.

Ethnicity serves as a third way of categorizing. When we talk about ethnicity, we're talking about history.

Every person has a history. They belong to a family or multiple families. Those families lived in particular places at particular times around particular people. Stories from families get passed down from generation to generation. Waves of tragedy and success shape them. Ethnic communities form when people with common histories choose to identify with each other. They may label themselves as a particular nation, people, or tribe.

WHY ETHNICITY?

Throughout this study, we'll make *ethnicity* our focus for talking about these biblical passages, rather than race or culture. I have three reasons for doing this.

First, ethnicity is a major theme in the Bible. Race shows up little, and when it does it doesn't fit current usage of the concept. The Bible says much about culture but does not use the concepts of culture and ethnicity interchangeably. A study on culture would be a different study.

Second, talking about ethnicity is highly strategic. Conversations about race quickly fill with shame and anger. Cultural dialogue easily slips into space that is shallow or safe. But talking about ethnicity will lay the foundation to engage more deeply with race or with culture or—most importantly—with the God who is over it all.

Finally, I've been deeply transformed by Jesus as I've leaned into ethnicity in the Bible. I've found myself better able to love my family and my neighbors. I think differently about what it means to be a Christian. And I have a deeper appreciation for Jesus and his work in this world. I would love for you to have a similar experience.

God has something to say to us about ethnicity. Will we hear him?

SUGGESTIONS FOR INDIVIDUAL STUDY

1. As you begin each study, pray that God will speak to you through his Word.

2. Read the introduction to the study and respond to the personal reflection question or exercise. This is designed to help you focus on God and on the theme of the study.

3. Each study deals with a particular passage—so that you can delve into the author's meaning in that context. Read and reread the passage to be studied. The questions are written using the language of the New International Version, so you may wish to use that version of the Bible. The New Revised Standard Version is also recommended.

4. This is an inductive Bible study, designed to help you discover for yourself what Scripture is saying. The study includes three types of questions. *Observation* questions ask about the basic facts: who, what, when, where, and how. *Interpretation* questions delve into the meaning of the passage. *Application* questions help you discover the implications of the text for growing in Christ. These three keys unlock the treasures of Scripture.

Write your answers to the questions in the spaces provided or in a personal journal. Writing can bring clarity and deeper understanding of yourself and of God's Word.

5. It might be good to have a Bible dictionary handy. Use it to look up any unfamiliar words, names, or places.

6. Use the prayer suggestion to guide you in thanking God for what you have learned and to pray about the applications that have come to mind.

7. You may want to go on to the suggestion under "Now or Later," or you may want to use that idea for your next study.

SUGGESTIONS FOR MEMBERS OF A GROUP STUDY

1. Come to the study prepared. Follow the suggestions for individual study mentioned above. You will find that careful preparation will greatly enrich your time spent in group discussion.

2. Be willing to participate in the discussion. The leader of your group will not be lecturing. Instead, he or she will be encouraging the members of the group to discuss what they have learned. The leader will be asking the questions that are found in this guide.

3. Stick to the topic being discussed. Your answers should be based on the verses which are the focus of the discussion and not on outside authorities such as commentaries or speakers. These studies focus on a particular passage of Scripture. Only rarely should you refer to other portions of the Bible. This allows for everyone to participate in in-depth study on equal ground.

4. Be sensitive to the other members of the group. Listen attentively when they describe what they have learned. You may be surprised by their insights! Each question assumes a variety of answers. Many questions do not have "right" answers, particularly questions that aim at meaning or application. Instead the questions push us to explore the passage more thoroughly.

When possible, link what you say to the comments of others. Also, be affirming whenever you can. This will encourage some of the more hesitant members of the group to participate.

5. Be careful not to dominate the discussion. We are sometimes so eager to express our thoughts that we leave too little opportunity for others to respond. By all means participate! But allow others to also.

6. Expect God to teach you through the passage being discussed and through the other members of the group. Pray that you will have an enjoyable and profitable time together, but also that as a result of the study you will find ways that you can take action individually and/or as a group.

7. Remember that anything said in the group is considered confidential and should not be discussed outside the group unless specific permission is given to do so.

8. If you are the group leader, you will find additional suggestions at the back of the guide.

ONE

FROM THE BEGINNING

Genesis 1:26-28; 11:1-9

Y ou have a history and belong to a family. We all do. Your ethnic identity emerges out of your history and your family. For some of us, our ethnic identities fill us with tension. Others navigate the world with little awareness of our ethnicity. Still others love our heritage. But how does God feel about ethnicity?

In this study, we'll see God's intention for humanity to "fill the earth" and "scatter." Diverse ethnic communities would inevitably form as humans lived in different places and developed their own unique histories. We are ethnic by design.

Group Discussion. In what ways are you grateful for diversity in your own life experience?

Personal Reflection. How would you describe your ethnic heritage? Try to come up with ten descriptive words.

The text features a poetic account of God's creation of humanity and his earliest blessing spoken over us. *Read Genesis 1:26-28.*

1. Ancient Hebrew poetry often used repetition to signal significance. What words, phrases, images, or ideas are repeated in this passage?

2. In what ways do you think those words or ideas have been twisted and used in ways God didn't intend them to be used?

3. What might be two or three reasons God had for giving humanity these particular commands?

4. This text takes place before the fall of humanity and the introduction of sin, brokenness, and evil into the human experience (Genesis 3). How might this fact shape our hopes and expectations of our experience of ethnic identity?

5. In what ways has your own ethnic identity felt like a blessing to you?

6. In what ways has your own ethnic identity felt like a burden to you?

Genesis 11 shows humanity's attempt to reject God's mandate for them. *Read Genesis 11:1-9.*

7. In 11:1-4, we see humanity united with one language, a common speech, and a shared purpose. What do you think it would feel like to live in a community like that? What would you find difficult or appealing?

8. What reasons might the people of the city have had for building the tower?

9. In 11:6-8 God confuses their language and scatters the people. What is your initial emotional response to God's action? Why do you think this is?

10. What reasons does the text give for God's intervention?

11. What evils arise when people attempt to maintain ethnic uniformity at all costs? Try to think of two to three examples from human history or your personal experience.

12. What social and spiritual benefits might arise from having multiple ethnic communities present in the world?

13. If ethnic diversity stems from God's original mandate and has been preserved by God, we should not be surprised to find material relating to ethnicity throughout the Bible. What benefits do you think you might receive from being more attuned to what God has to say about ethnicity?

 Ask God to open your ears to what he has to say about ethnicity in his Word.

||||||||||||||||||||||||||| NOW OR LATER |||||||||||||||||||||||||||||

As we engage in a study of ethnicity in the Bible, we will at times have to dig a little deeper into our own presuppositions and experiences of ethnicity. The following prayer exercise offers support for this process. You might want to return to it regularly as you study.

Find a relaxing place to sit or lie down.

Take a deep breath in and hold it for a few seconds.

Breathe out and, as you exhale, pray, "Lord, I need your help . . ."

As you breathe back in, share where you need help. Use the following prompts or add your own:

- "to hear you clearly"
- "to love my family"
- "to feel like I belong"
- "to heal from my past"
- "to be open-minded"

When you're ready to move on, close your eyes and say, "Thank you, Lord."

TWO

ETHNIC ON PURPOSE

Genesis 12:1-5

W hen preaching in Athens, the apostle Paul declared that God "made all the nations, that they should inhabit the whole earth; and he marked out their appointed times in history and the boundaries of their lands. God did this so that they would seek him and perhaps reach out for him and find him, though he is not far from any one of us" (Acts 17:26-27). Paul felt convinced that God created ethnicity. God did this on purpose.

Where would Paul get these ideas? From his youth, Paul had heard Scriptures that taught that God chooses to work through ethnic identity and ethnic communities to bring the most remarkable blessings into the world. Today's passage would have been one that shaped generations of students of Scripture.

Group Discussion. What positive and negative narratives do people have about your ethnic community? Share what you've heard and how it's affected you.

Personal Reflection. What do you love most about your ethnic communities? What does your people have that you wish everyone could see and know?

Genesis 12 recounts how and why God called Abram out of Ur of the Chaldeans to form a new ethnic community. *Read Genesis 12:1-5.*

1. What would you expect to happen to Abram's family over time if they journeyed away from his country, people, and father's household?

2. How is your experience of your ethnicity different from your ancestors'?

3. In verse 2, the Lord says he will make Abram and his descendants into a distinct nation. How do you think Abram would have felt to hear this?

4. From this passage, what did God intend to do through this new ethnic community?

5. Using what you've picked up of the biblical narrative over the years, in what ways did Abram's descendants ultimately bless all peoples on earth?

6. In what ways do your ethnic communities bless the people around you?

7. How does this make you feel about your ethnic identity?

8. In what ways have you been blessed by ethnic communities to which you don't belong?

9. How can you express gratitude for those blessings?

10. What steps can you take this week to share a blessing from your ethnic community with someone outside of it?

11. What steps can you take this week to actively, graciously, and gratefully receive a blessing being offered from someone from a different ethnic community?

 Take some time right now to write out your action steps and to write out a prayer of gratitude to God. If you're doing this study with a group, read your prayers aloud as you offer them to the Lord.

||||||||||||||||||||||||||||| NOW OR LATER |||||||||||||||||||||||||||||||||||

Many of us struggle to identify ways our ethnic communities bless the broader world. We're afraid to sound arrogant or supremacist. Or we just lack the insight. The following focused interview practice may help.

Identify two to three people of your own ethnic communities. Ask to interview them about their heritage for fifteen to thirty minutes. Ask the following questions, listen respectfully, and take notes.

- What five words would you use to describe our ethnic community?
- What do you admire about our community?
- What do you wish other people knew about our community?
- What gifts does our community bring to the world?

This exercise can be particularly challenging for white Americans. I've found chapter 12 of *Being White* by Paula Harris and Doug Schaupp to be helpful for people struggling with this exercise.

THREE

OUR BROKEN ETHNIC STORIES

Exodus 2:11–3:12

God created each of us with a longing to belong. We want to belong in our families, our friendship networks, and sometimes our ethnic communities. This makes our experiences of rejection and exclusion feel remarkably painful.

As we engage with what the Bible has to say about ethnic identity, we discover that our broader communities influence how we identify. Those communities can give us permission to identify with them or they can deny us access. They can make us want to identify with them or can make us want to pass as part of a different community. Some of us might also belong to multiple ethnic communities at the same time.

In the midst of all of this, the Lord calls us into community with himself. He even does this *through* our families, our friendship networks, and our ethnic communities. Though each of those relationships can carry pain and brokenness, they also can become places where we meet God.

Group Discussion. When have you felt like you didn't fit or want to fit in your ethnic community?

Personal Reflection. Imagine what it would feel like to be rejected by your ethnic community. What would you feel like you'd lost?

Moses was born into a Hebrew family during the period when the Israelites had been enslaved in Egypt for generations. Moses, however, ended up being adopted by the Pharaoh's family and raised with Egyptian privilege. *Read Exodus 2:11–3:12.*

1. How does the text mention Moses' ethnicity?

2. What impact might the competing narratives of Moses' identity have had on his sense of belonging?

3. What are some competing narratives around your own ethnic identity?

4. How might a desire to belong to or distance oneself from an ethnic community drive a person's behavior? Try to think of two to three examples from your own life or from others.

5. Where do you see points of conflict in the passage?

6. How does ethnicity play into those conflicts?

7. In what ways might Moses' sense of connection or disconnection with his ethnic communities have fueled his behavior?

8. What are other ways Moses could have responded to the abuse he saw in verse 11?

9. Why did Moses choose murder? What was he hoping would happen?

10. When you think about the ethnic communities to which you belong, where do you see brokenness?

11. Twice in the text we're told that God sees, hears, and feels concern over the Hebrews' situation. At the same time, Moses is a failed revolutionary who is passing as an Egyptian in exile in Midian. Why would God include Moses in the task of liberating the Israelites?

12. When Moses asks, "Who am I?" God responds with, "I will be with you." How might God's presence with you empower you to engage your ethnic identity?

13. How might God use your unique ethnic background to prepare you for a particular way of serving or ministering in his kingdom?

 Ask God to give you eyes to see the ways he's prepared you to serve and minister. Ask him to bring healing and hope to your ethnic community.

||||||||||||||||||||||||||| NOW OR LATER |||||||||||||||||||||||||||||

AAA exercise. We each carry beauty and brokenness into the world. How can we seek healing?

Step 1: Acknowledge. Don't hide your hurt. Bring your pain to the surface in a journal or speak it aloud. Describe it to God.

Step 2: Ask. What do you want God to do for you and your community? Make your request directly to God.

Step 3: Act. God loves to include us in his work of redemption, just as he included Moses. Listen to God's Spirit and do what he invites you to do.

Wounds to our ethnic identities and in our ethnic communities cut to the deepest parts of us. We need the Lord to bring the redemption, rescue, and healing for which our hearts long.

Additional Scripture. Moses continues to wrestle with his ethnic identity and his calling as a prophet. Read the full context of the passage (Exodus 1–4) with an eye for ethnic brokenness, and you'll discover Pharaoh's racism, Moses' insecurity, and the Lord's persistence to bring healing to both Moses and his ethnic communities.

FOUR

NAVIGATING PRESSURE TO ASSIMILATE

Daniel 1:1-21

Human beings come hardwired with a desire to fit in somewhere. We long to belong. Yet this can be difficult, as we saw in the last study. We all face pressures to discard or bury some aspects of our identities in an attempt to smooth out the differences between us and the people around us. Social scientists refer to this as "assimilation."

Two things happen when we attempt to assimilate: we pick up wounds to our identities, and we lose out on blessings that God has for us (and the people around us). The painful truth about our attempts to assimilate is that they always fail. God is the one who made us; we lack the power to remake ourselves. He can redeem every ethnic heritage and empower each of us to thrive.

Group Discussion. When have you been immersed in a community of people who were different from you? How did your behavior change in this environment?

Personal Reflection. What would you say are the nonnegotiable elements of your ethnic identity? In what ways have you been pressured to hide or discard these?

The book of Daniel starts at the beginning of the Babylonian exile, when the people of Judah have been conquered by King Nebuchadnezzar and have lost their independence. In this passage, we'll see how a group of young Israelite men navigated the pressure to assimilate. *Read Daniel 1:1-21.*

1. In verses 3-5, what do we learn about the young Israelites?

2. Why do you think the king took these men into his service?

3. Where do you see the young Israelites being pressured to assimilate?

4. Look at the giving of new names in verse 7. What impact would these new names have had on the young men?

5. In what ways have people tried to "name" or "rename" you? How did that experience affect you?

6. Why did Daniel resolve not to eat the royal food and wine?

7. We sometimes believe that fitting in is the only way to thrive. Share some examples of this myth from your own life or in the world around you.

8. What are ways you can "test" or practice resistance to assimilation in your own life?

9. What do we see God doing in this passage?

10. Why might the author have wanted us to see these instances of God at work in the midst of this situation?

11. Daniel and his friends resolved not to assimilate with the food and wine, but they actively engaged with the language and literature of Babylon. How do you think they made that decision?

12. What factors might you use when deciding whether to adapt or assimilate in a given situation? Make a case study for yourself.

13. The unnamed guard in the passage is easily overlooked. But his willingness to risk giving Daniel and his friends space to experiment made a huge impact on this story. In what ways can you help create space for others to experiment with resisting assimilation?

Pause to ask God to give you wisdom as you navigate pressures to assimilate and compassion for those who face a different set of pressures than your own.

NOW OR LATER

Our healthiest decisions come when we listen to and follow the God who made us, placed us in our families of origin, and sent us out into the diverse world in which we live. The following exercise is designed to help you grow in your capacity to hear and obey God.

- Take a few moments to settle quietly into your body and into God's welcome of you. Breathe. Close your eyes if that helps. God cares deeply for you and wants you to know him.
- When you're ready, read Romans 12:1-6 out loud slowly.
- Ask Jesus to show you which gifts he's given you in your ethnic identity that you're being tempted to discard. Ask him to show you what he wants you to do.
- Take some time to write down what you hear from God.
- When listening to God, we always want to hold what we hear with humility. Compare what you're hearing with Scripture. Share it with a mature friend. Do you feel peace?

If what you're hearing aligns with the Bible, sounds wise to a mature friend, and doesn't cause unhealthy fear, go for it and be blessed.

FIVE

ETHNICITY AND THE GOSPEL OF CHRIST

Ephesians 2:1-22

How do we show that the gospel has power? We can point to changed lives, including our personal stories of redemption and transformation. We might talk about the influence of Jesus on society over the centuries: the rise of hospitals and universities, the abolitionist movement and the social pressure against infanticide, the move to consider humility and forgiveness as virtues.

But if you read Paul's epistles, you might be surprised to find that he reaches for one thing over and over again to demonstrate that the gospel has power: the presence of a multiethnic church. Much of Paul's writing in the New Testament focuses on how the gospel of Jesus Christ makes multiethnic churches possible.

Despite this, in much of modern times the hours when churches gather have remained the most segregated. Our failure to live in multiethnic community turns the volume down on our witness to a watching world. And we also miss out on the blessings God wants to bring us through each other.

Group Discussion. If someone asked you, what would you point them to in order to show that the gospel has power?

Personal Reflection. What barriers do you see to multiethnic community? Make a list.

This study's text captures what might be Paul's clearest and most objective description of the good news about Jesus Christ. *Read Ephesians 2:1-22.*

1. What do you find to be the most beautiful phrase or image in this passage?

2. What do you consider the most challenging phrase or image in this passage?

3. What does this passage tell us about salvation?

4. How might this message have been received differently by people of different ethnic backgrounds (Jews and Gentiles)?

5. According to Paul, how does the gospel change how both Jews and Gentiles interact with God?

6. How does it change the way Jews and Gentiles interact with each other?

7. God has an active role in building a multiethnic community. Why do you think he cares about this?

8. When you first learned about the gospel, what role did ethnic reconciliation and multiethnic community play in what you heard?

9. What effect did this inclusion or exclusion have on your expectations for ethnic reconciliation and multiethnic community in the church?

10. Many in our society today long to see peace between ethnic communities and the formation of truly inclusive multiethnic communities. How might multiethnic churches meet this longing?

11. What divisions need to come down in your communities for ethnically diverse peoples to live at peace with each other?

Take some time to pray that Jesus would continue to tear down the divisions between peoples in your community. He is the source of multiethnic community and our best hope. Won't he do it?

▌▌▌▌▌▌▌▌▌▌▌▌▌▌▌▌▌▌▌▌▌ NOW OR LATER ▌▌▌▌▌▌▌▌▌▌▌▌▌▌▌▌▌▌▌▌▌▌▌

We want to lay a solid theological foundation for multiethnic community. This was also a significant project for the early church. Much of the writing that came to be included in the New Testament directly or indirectly focuses on this foundation-building work. Yet few of us have been trained to hear this.

Read or listen to Galatians or Romans. How does Paul's talk about the gospel point toward multiethnic community?

SIX

UNITY THROUGH DIVERSITY

Acts 6:1-7

Over the last several studies we've seen that ethnicity comes from God as a blessing. That blessing, however, has been complicated by our human brokenness and has become a source of pain for many of us. We need God to heal us. And as we're healed, God invites us to bring our healthy, whole selves into our Christian communities— communities marked by diversity.

As we grow in awareness about ethnicity in the Bible, we'll notice in new ways how ethnicity shows up in our communities. We might become attentive to the presence or absence of diversity in our churches. We might pay closer attention to the ways ethnicity affects power dynamics. We might also tune into ongoing conflicts between ethnic groups.

How can we live into our growing awareness in a healthy way?

Group Discussion. Where have you experienced leadership from someone from your own ethnic background, and where have you experienced it from someone from a different ethnic background? What kind of influence does this have on your picture of leadership?

Personal Reflection. Take a look at a recent conflict you've experienced. What role did ethnicity play? Consider how ethnicity shaped how the conflict was communicated, navigated, and resolved. (This particular conflict doesn't have to be around ethnicity or across ethnic lines; since every person has an ethnic identity, ethnicity shows up in every conflict.)

Our text for this study captures a significant conflict in the early church. Thousands of people have come to faith in Christ. All of the believers remain in Jerusalem. Although at this point they all are Jewish, they come from different ethnic backgrounds. Some have stronger Greek roots than others. It's in this context that the conflict appears. *Read Acts 6:1-7.*

1. What was the conflict about in this text?

2. Why do you think Luke, the writer of Acts, gave the ethnic contours of this particular conflict?

3. Where have you experienced conflict in ethnically diverse communities?

4. Why do you think the Hellenistic or Greek-origin Jewish widows were being overlooked?

5. Come up with three unhealthy ways the Twelve *could* have responded to the complaint. Have fun with it!

6. What impact would those unhealthy responses have had on the community?

7. In what ways have you seen unhealthy responses in your own experiences of diverse community?

8. What impact did those responses have on you and the unity of your community?

9. The seven "servants" or "deacons" all turn out to have Greek names. This leads many commentators to believe that the apostles placed a group of Hellenistic Jews in charge of distributing the food to all the widows in the community. Why do you think they made that choice?

10. Even the Twelve struggled to navigate multiethnic spaces. But the Holy Spirit continued to work mercifully and give them opportunities to grow. Take a moment to write out places in your cross-ethnic relationships where you have needed or seen the Spirit's mercy.

11. After this resolution, many people come to faith, including a large number of priests. How might the believers' response have been a witness to those watching the community from its edges?

12. What can you do this week to share your power and authority with someone who is being overlooked?

13. Where in your life do you need to speak up (as did the people who made the complaint) or step up (as did the seven Hellenistic deacons)?

 Ask God to help you live, love, and serve in healthy ways as you join his work in building a missional multiethnic community.

NOW OR LATER

Make a four-column list. In one column list your five closest friends. In the next list the last ten people with whom you've had a meaningful interaction (for example, a conversation lasting more than ten minutes or an intense emotional engagement). In the third list people who have some social, spiritual, or vocational authority over you. In the final column list people over whom you have some social, spiritual, or vocational authority. The same people may show up on multiple lists, or one of the lists may be empty. That's okay.

Note the ethnic identity of each person on your lists. For example, if the author of this study was on your list, you'd note "White and

Cuban-American." If you don't know someone's ethnic identity, write "unknown."

What trends do you notice in your lists? Where do you see diversity or a lack of diversity? What would you like to see change?

Consider a recent conflict with someone on the list. What role did ethnicity play in that conflict? In what ways was this healthy or unhealthy?

Reflect on how social systems and structures shape your lists and interactions. These often operate in the background of our lives. Bring them to the foreground and ask the Lord: "What would you have me seek to change in order to participate more fully in the multiethnic community you're forming in the world?"

SEVEN

ENGAGING ETHNIC TENSION

Matthew 15:21-28

A s we near the end of these studies, you now have a chance to
pull together everything you've learned about ethnicity as you
engage one of the most challenging texts in the Bible. In this passage,
Jesus says things that many readers and commentators find surprising,
disturbing, or shocking.

Yet Jesus stands at the center of all Christian theology; therefore, we
need him to stand at the center of our thinking about ethnicity in the Bible.
We need to allow him to adjust all of our expectations and categories.

As you read, keep the following truths about Jesus in mind:

- He is the image of the invisible God. (Colossians 1:15)
- He had no sin. (2 Corinthians 5:21)
- He came to destroy barriers between people and to give all ethnic
  communities access to God. (Ephesians 2:14-18)

Group Discussion. What has been a recent challenging interaction
you've had across ethnic lines? What made it so challenging?

Personal Reflection. When you think about Jesus' ethnic identity, what
comes to mind? How does this align with images of Jesus you've seen
or grown up with?

Matthew's Gospel presents Jesus as a distinctly Jewish Messiah: de-
scended from Abraham and David, fulfilling prophecy, and inaugu-
rating the kingdom of heaven. Throughout Jesus' life and ministry,
conflicts with religious and governmental authorities arise. We also see
ethnic tension (even in Jesus' mixed genealogy).

Our text for this study takes place in the region of Tyre and Sidon: prosperous Roman port cities, the historical home of the Canaanites, and the site of ancient stories of Jewish-Gentile partnership. In this area, Jesus and his disciples would have been surrounded by people from many different heritages. *Read Matthew 15:21-28.*

1. How does ethnicity show up in this text?

2. Why do you think Jesus needed an ethnic identity?

3. What responses does the Canaanite woman receive when she calls out to Jesus?

4. What reasons might Jesus have had for not immediately responding to the woman?

5. From your ethnic background, what layers of meaning get attached when someone doesn't respond immediately to a request?

6. How does your ethnic heritage affect your perception of good, loving, or kind behavior? Try to think of a few examples.

7. The interaction here shows no "colorblindness." What new opportunities are available to Jesus and the Canaanite woman when they acknowledge their different ethnic identities?

8. What has been your personal experience when people acknowledge ethnic differences?

9. In verse 26, instead of running from the cross-ethnic tension, Jesus leans into the conversation and increases the tension. Why might he have done this?

10. When have you directly engaged a tension like this? What was the result?

11. What do Jesus and the Canaanite woman do to transform the cross-ethnic tension into something healing?

12. As the passage ends, we hear Jesus praise the woman's faith (affirming her agency) and give her daughter healing (actually assisting). In the context of ethnic tension, what difference does it make for these two to go together?

13. How might witnessing this encounter affect your views of your own ethnic identity?

How might it affect your willingness to acknowledge the ethnic identities of others?

How might it affect your ways of responding to cross-ethnic tension?

NOW OR LATER

Jesus navigated a world full of ethnic identities and tension. Although he didn't live a conflict-free life in this arena, he was always able to love. I hope that, after participating in this study, you will find yourself better able to love: to love your own ethnic identity, to love across ethnic lines, and to live in a loving way in your personal relationships and in the structures and systems in which you find yourself.

One helpful exercise on this journey is the disciple of celebration. Grab a journal and some free time and complete the following reflections:

- When I started this study . . .
- Today, I can see that God has been growing me in the following ways . . .
- Now, I'm better able to share the following blessings with my community . . .

End your time by celebrating God's good work in and through you. He brought you to this conversation—in this season—for a reason. He sees and knows you. He wants the best for you. He wants to include you in his beloved community. And through all of who you are, there's good that he wants to do.

EIGHT

ETHNIC FOREVER

Revelation 7:9-17

Y our ethnic identity will never expire. The same is true for people who are different from you. We will be ethnic forever in the presence of God.

Today we live in a world full of ethnic conflict, of painful attempts at colorblindness, of assimilation and segregation. Yet we carry in us the hope of a redeemed world. Unity is our destiny. We will gather together in all our diversity to worship the God who made each of us unique.

We need this vision of the future to navigate our present. Our hope for our ethnic identities and multiethnic communities comes from Jesus Christ, who holds our futures in his hands.

Group Discussion. What do you think a fully redeemed, healthy multiethnic community would be like? How would it feel to be part of a community like that?

Personal Reflection. Where have you felt hopeless when it comes to ethnic reconciliation and multiethnic community? Share your feelings with Jesus and ask him to give you reasons to hope again: "I hope. Help me to hope!"

This text comes from the apostle John, who received this vision when he lived in exile on the isle of Patmos. At the time, the church was experiencing severe persecution. They felt desperate for hope. *Read Revelation 7:9-17.*

1. How would you describe this scene?

2. What do all the people have in common?

3. How might John have known that the people were from every nation, tribe, people, and language?

4. What ethnic distinctives does it seem (from this text) might some day pass away?

5. What ethnic distinctives does it seem (again, from this text) might remain forever?

6. What reasons could God have for preserving our distinct ethnic identities forever?

7. How might the permanence of our ethnic identities affect how we engage them in the here and now?

8. The passage acknowledges the suffering of all these ethnic communities, including their tears. Take a few moments to write out some of that pain from your own communities and hold it up to God, recognizing that God sees, knows, and cares.

9. What would it mean for your ethnic community to be healed and safe?

10. Knowing that at least some facets of our ethnic identities will last forever, what one step of learning can you take to more deeply engage your ethnic identities this week?

11. What one step of service can you take this week to join God in his work of wiping away tears and bringing healing?

12. What one step of witness can you take this week to let someone know that their ethnic identity is something treasured enough by God to last forever?

Thank God for your various ethnic identities. Ask him to help you steward them well in the present so they can be used to glorify him now and forever.

NOW OR LATER

Have you ever experienced multiethnic worship? Worship in different languages and diverse styles can help us appreciate the eternal gift God is giving us as he forms a church from every nation, tribe, people, and language.

For an example, check out the *Urbana 18 Live: Faithful Witness* album. You can listen to it for free on Spotify or purchase it almost anywhere music is sold online. The album contains worship songs in multiple languages and in styles associated with various ethnic communities. The musicians also come from diverse ethnic backgrounds. Listen to the album and worship the Lord wholeheartedly.

LEADER'S NOTES

My grace is sufficient for you.

2 CORINTHIANS 12:9

L eading a Bible discussion can be an enjoyable and rewarding experience. But it can also be *scary*—especially if you've never done it before. If this is your feeling, you're in good company. When God asked Moses to lead the Israelites out of Egypt, he replied, "O Lord, please send someone else to do it" (Exodus 4:13). It was the same with Solomon, Jeremiah, and Timothy, but God helped these people in spite of their weaknesses, and he will help you as well.

You don't need to be an expert on the Bible or a trained teacher to lead a Bible discussion. The idea behind these inductive studies is that the leader guides group members to discover for themselves what the Bible has to say. This method of learning will allow group members to remember much more of what is said than a lecture would.

These studies are designed to be led easily. As a matter of fact, the flow of questions through the passage from observation to interpretation to application is so natural that you may feel that the studies lead themselves. This study guide is also flexible. You can use it with a variety of groups—student, professional, neighborhood, or church groups. Each study takes forty-five to sixty minutes in a group setting.

There are some important facts to know about group dynamics and encouraging discussion. The suggestions listed below should enable you to effectively and enjoyably fulfill your role as leader.

PREPARING FOR THE STUDY

1. Ask God to help you understand and apply the passage in your own life. Unless this happens, you will not be prepared to lead others. Pray too for the various members of the group. Ask God to open your hearts to the message of his Word and motivate you to action.

2. Read the introduction to the entire guide to get an overview of the entire book and the issues which will be explored.

3. As you begin each study, read and reread the assigned Bible passage to familiarize yourself with it.

4. This study guide is based on the New International Version of the Bible. It will help you and the group if you use this translation as the basis for your study and discussion.

5. Carefully work through each question in the study. Spend time in meditation and reflection as you consider how to respond.

6. Write your thoughts and responses in the space provided in the study guide. This will help you to express your understanding of the passage clearly.

7. It might help to have a Bible dictionary handy. Use it to look up any unfamiliar words, names, or places. (For additional help on how to study a passage, see chapter five of *How to Lead a LifeBuilder Study*, IVP, 2018.)

8. Consider how you can apply the Scripture to your life. Remember that the group will follow your lead in responding to the studies. They will not go any deeper than you do.

9. Once you have finished your own study of the passage, familiarize yourself with the leader's notes for the study you are leading. These are designed to help you in several ways. First, they tell you the purpose the study guide author had in mind when writing the study. Take time to think through how the study questions work together to accomplish that purpose. Second, the notes provide you with additional background information or suggestions on group dynamics for various questions. This information can be useful when people have difficulty understanding or answering a question. Third, the leader's notes can alert you to potential problems you may encounter during the study.

10. If you wish to remind yourself of anything mentioned in the leader's notes, make a note to yourself below that question in the study.

LEADING THE STUDY

1. Begin the study on time. Open with prayer, asking God to help the group to understand and apply the passage.

2. Be sure that everyone in your group has a study guide. Encourage the group to prepare beforehand for each discussion by reading the introduction to the guide and by working through the questions in the study.

3. At the beginning of your first time together, explain that these studies are meant to be discussions, not lectures. Encourage the members of the group to participate. However, do not put pressure on those who may be hesitant to speak during the first few sessions. You may want to suggest the following guidelines to your group.

- Stick to the topic being discussed.
- Your responses should be based on the verses which are the focus of the discussion and not on outside authorities such as commentaries or speakers.
- These studies focus on a particular passage of Scripture. Only rarely should you refer to other portions of the Bible. This allows for everyone to participate in in-depth study on equal ground.
- Anything said in the group is considered confidential and will not be discussed outside the group unless specific permission is given to do so.
- We will listen attentively to each other and provide time for each person present to talk.
- We will pray for each other.

4. Have a group member read the introduction at the beginning of the discussion.

5. Every session begins with a group discussion question. The question or activity is meant to be used before the passage is read. The question introduces the theme of the study and encourages group members to begin to open up. Encourage as many members as possible to participate, and be ready to get the discussion going with your own response.

This section is designed to reveal where our thoughts or feelings need to be transformed by Scripture. That is why it is especially important not to read the passage before the discussion question is asked. The passage will tend to color the honest reactions people would otherwise give because they are, of course, supposed to think the way the Bible does.

You may want to supplement the group discussion question with an icebreaker to help people to get comfortable. See the community section of the *Small Group Starter Kit* (IVP, 1995) for more ideas.

You also might want to use the personal reflection question with your group. Either allow a time of silence for people to respond individually or discuss it together.

6. Have a group member (or members if the passage is long) read aloud the passage to be studied. Then give people several minutes to read the passage again silently so that they can take it all in.

7. Question 1 will generally be an overview question designed to briefly survey the passage. Encourage the group to look at the whole passage, but try to avoid getting sidetracked by questions or issues that will be addressed later in the study.

8. As you ask the questions, keep in mind that they are designed to be used just as they are written. You may simply read them aloud. Or you may prefer to express them in your own words.

There may be times when it is appropriate to deviate from the study guide. For example, a question may have already been answered. If so, move on to the next question. Or someone may raise an important question not covered in the guide. Take time to discuss it, but try to keep the group from going off on tangents.

9. Avoid answering your own questions. If necessary, repeat or rephrase them until they are clearly understood. Or point out something you read in the leader's notes to clarify the context or meaning. An eager group quickly becomes passive and silent if they think the leader will do most of the talking.

10. Don't be afraid of silence. People may need time to think about the question before formulating their answers.

11. Don't be content with just one answer. Ask, "What do the rest of you think?" or "Anything else?" until several people have given answers to the question.

12. Acknowledge all contributions. Try to be affirming whenever possible. Never reject an answer. If it is clearly off-base, ask, "Which verse led you to that conclusion?" or again, "What do the rest of you think?"

13. Don't expect every answer to be addressed to you, even though this will probably happen at first. As group members become more at ease, they will begin to truly interact with each other. This is one sign of healthy discussion.

14. Don't be afraid of controversy. It can be very stimulating. If you don't resolve an issue completely, don't be frustrated. Move on and keep it in mind for later. A subsequent study may solve the problem.

15. Periodically summarize what the group has said about the passage. This helps to draw together the various ideas mentioned and gives continuity to the study. But don't preach.

16. At the end of the Bible discussion you may want to allow group members a time of quiet to work on an idea under "Now or Later." Then discuss what you experienced. Or you may want to encourage group members to work on these ideas between meetings. Give an opportunity during the session for people to talk about what they are learning.

17. Conclude your time together with conversational prayer, adapting the prayer suggestion at the end of the study to your group. Ask for God's help in following through on the commitments you've made.

18. End on time.

Many more suggestions and helps are found in *How to Lead a LifeBuilder Study.*

COMPONENTS OF SMALL GROUPS

A healthy small group should do more than study the Bible. There are four components to consider as you structure your time together.

Nurture. Small groups help us to grow in our knowledge and love of God. Bible study is the key to making this happen and is the foundation of your small group.

Community. Small groups are a great place to develop deep friendships with other Christians. Allow time for informal interaction before and after each study. Plan activities and games that will help you get to know each other. Spend time having fun together—going on a picnic or cooking dinner together.

Worship and prayer. Your study will be enhanced by spending time praising God together in prayer or song. Pray for each other's needs—and keep track of how God is answering prayer in your group. Ask God to help you to apply what you are learning in your study.

Outreach. Reaching out to others can be a practical way of applying what you are learning, and it will keep your group from becoming self-focused. Host a series of evangelistic discussions for your friends or neighbors. Clean up the yard of an elderly friend. Serve at a soup kitchen together, or spend a day working in the community.

Many more suggestions and helps in each of these areas are found in the *Small Group Starter Kit.* You will also find information on building a small group. Reading through the starter kit will be worth your time.

STUDY 1. FROM THE BEGINNING. GENESIS 1:26-28; 11:1-9

PURPOSE: To reveal God's hand in creating a multiethnic humanity.

Question 1. Notice "image of God"—both an ontological ("like God") and functional ("made to rule") creation, according to Philip Hughes in *The True Image*; "created"; "rule over."

Question 2. Not all human beings have treated those beyond their particular ethnic community as if they were also created in God's image. The command to have dominion has been used to justify abuse of creation and subjugation of people who were considered inferior. The language of this mandate has been used to normalize a certain kind of family life (married with lots of kids) and to shame those called to singleness or to a broader picture of family life (particularly a tribal life).

Question 3. The work of filling and ruling over the earth needed doing (often called the "cultural mandate"); they were uniquely suited to this work; God thought they'd enjoy doing the work; it could help them grow into maturity; it created space for relationships with God and with each other.

Question 4. Ethnicity is not inherently opposed to unity; it is not bad or evil. If sinful human beings can have an ethnic identity, Jesus can have one too. And our ethnic identities might be able to be redeemed and restored to their original purpose by Jesus.

Question 7. Reflecting on this question can give you space for your own presuppositions to come to the surface. Maybe you'll see a desire for colorblindness. Or maybe such a uniform community would feel like a nightmare to you. There are no right or wrong answers.

Question 8. The text offers two reasons: to make a name for themselves (note that the name of this city before the scattering is never recorded); to prevent scattering (building skyscrapers instead of suburbs, perhaps).

Adding personal experience and the broader biblical context might also allow us to explore other theories: direct rebellion against the cultural mandate of Genesis 1; wanting to determine their own fate; ethnic hegemony, mono-ethnicity, or a fear of growing diversity. Also, this passage comes right after the narrative of the great flood, and they use waterproof tar for mortar on their tower. Do they not trust God to keep his promise to never flood the earth again?

Question 9. One response might be frustration: "I long to see people come together, but God is scattering them." Another example might be relief: "I've lived in places where the norm was to conform, and it's stifling."

Question 10. If they aren't scattered, nothing they plan will be impossible for them; preventing understanding leads to scattering (a return to the cultural mandate).

Question 11. Failure to represent people from diverse ethnic backgrounds in media leads to continued discrimination and entrenchment of negative stereotypes. The Holocaust is an extreme example. A personal example might sound like, "I've had my job threatened because I failed to code switch and it made my supervisor uncomfortable."

Question 12. If we're all created in God's image, then a diverse humanity might help us know God better as we see more of his complex glory on display. Other people might pick up on biblical themes that we'd miss because we don't share their history or experiences. The experience of uniting across differences to accomplish a goal or purpose might add another layer of beauty to our work in the world.

Question 13. We might receive healing in areas where our ethnic identity has been painful. We might discover new ways to be inclusive and to love. "There is within Christianity a breathtakingly powerful way to imagine and enact the social, to imagine and enact connection and belonging" (Willie James Jennings, *The Christian Imagination: Theology and the Origins of Race* [New Haven, CT: Yale University Press, 2010], 4). We might find ways to speak evangelistically into deeply held values of our society. We might discover healthier foundations for cross-ethnic relationships than the guilt/shame/duty motivations that often fuel these attempts in society. "Ethnic identity gives us a sense of belonging and a place that's unique. God created us uniquely and that should be honored" (Leroy Barber, *Embrace* [Downers Grove, IL: InterVarsity Press, 2016], 51).

STUDY 2. ETHNIC ON PURPOSE. GENESIS 12:1-5

PURPOSE: To see ethnicity as a gift and a blessing.

Question 1. Following the previous study on Genesis 1 and the cultural mandate, we might expect moving away from one's particular ethnic community to over time create differentiation and, potentially, a distinct ethnic identity. For example, some of the author's family immigrated to the United States from Cuba, and after several generations they now have a Cuban-American identity that is distinct in many ways from a Cuban ethnic identity. Other potential answers are: they might struggle as they move away from support systems; they might benefit as they interact more frequently with other ethnic communities; they might "lose their roots" or struggle to know what parts of their ethnic identities come from their Chaldean heritage.

Question 3. There are no wrong answers to this question. We ask questions like this to encourage reflection on the humanity of the people in the passages and to deepen our appreciation for their challenges and decisions. Possible answers include: gratitude, curiosity, fear, sadness, skepticism, hope, joy, frustration. If your group stalls here, you could pick two to three items from this list and have them discuss why (or why not) Abram might have felt this way.

Question 4. The covenant the Lord makes here contains promises both for Abram's descendants and for how those descendants will interact with other ethnic communities. The promises for what would become Israel are both general ("I will bless you") and specific ("I will make your name [reputation] great"). Through these people, the Lord would also "bless all peoples on earth." The Hebrew word for "peoples" here would have been resonant for Hebrew readers as it was used five times in the "Table of Nations" genealogies describing humanity after the flood (Genesis 10). Finally, "peoples" would indicate multiple ethnic communities, not just multiple individuals.

Question 5. Possible answers include: they stood as humanity's primary representatives in their interactions with the Lord for generations; they protected God's law, laying the ethical foundations of much of modern life; they challenged prevailing cultural notions for how women, children, immigrants, slaves, and the poor should be treated; they showed that humans continue to sin despite the best access to God and the strongest desire to live rightly with him; they served as the ethnic community of origin for both Jesus Christ and the Christian movement.

Note: I'm taking a step in this study to extend the ethnic-blessing logic of the covenant to the broader nations (including our own ethnic identities). This understanding comes from the breadth of Scripture, including passages we'll look at in later studies. That said, original hearers of this particular passage probably would not have recognized this broader perspective. This is one reason it's important to pause here and reflect on the particular gifts brought by the particular community with whom the Lord initiated these covenants.

Questions 6-11. I realize that these questions might present a particular challenge to our white American brothers and sisters. In *Pondering Privilege*, Jody Wiley Fernando suggests, "White people don't talk about race because they fear saying the wrong thing.... They have no idea how to enter a conversation about race because they've never had one" (Minneapolis, MN: NextStep, 2016, 45). For many white Americans, their ethnic identity is understood as "normal" and, as such, becomes invisible to them. There can also be social pressure against identifying any positive attribute with a white American ethnic identity.

The stakes are high. Sandra Maria van Opstal writes, "The biggest barrier Christians face in developing communities hospitable to people of every ethnicity and culture is their own ignorance about their own culture" (*The Next Worship* [Downers Grove, IL: InterVarsity Press, 2016], 40). Sarah Shin continues: "Colorblindness, though well intentioned, is inhospitable. Colorblindness assumes that we are similar enough and that we all only have good intentions, so we can avoid our differences" (*Beyond Colorblind* [Downers Grove, IL: InterVarsity Press, 2017], 6).

Here are some tips that can help you guide this discussion:

- If your group is struggling with this tension, name it. Encourage people to express their feelings about the discussion.

- Share the truth that positive ethnic attributes are neither exclusive nor comprehensive. An attribute may be present in many but not all members of an ethnic community. And that same attribute might also be present in other ethnic communities. For example, saying that white Americans value a high work ethic doesn't mean there aren't lazy white Americans or that Cuban Americans aren't hard working.

- Even if your group struggles to get through these questions, caution against naming stereotypes of other ethnic groups (even positive ones). There's a huge difference between using a generalization of your own community and having someone else do it.

- Be aware that you might be blessed with some ethnically mixed people in your group. They may feel some of these tensions in unique ways. Encourage them to share their perspective. They offer something to the conversation that's deeply valuable. As Virgilio Elizondo said: "Herein lies the contribution of the *mestizo* of today: to show in one's person that racial and cultural mixture does not have to be destructive of cultural identity, but that it can even strengthen it" (*The Future Is Mestizo* [Boulder, CO: University Press, 2000], 95).

STUDY 3. OUR BROKEN ETHNIC STORIES. EXODUS 2:11–3:12

PURPOSE: To seek and receive healing related to our ethnic identities.

Question 1. Moses is described as a Hebrew multiple times (emphasized in 2:11); Reuel's daughters describe Moses as an Egyptian (2:19); Moses describes himself as a foreigner in Midian (2:22); God describes Moses as being related to Abraham, Isaac, and Jacob (3:6).

Question 2. A significant portion of Moses' interaction with God in Exodus 3–4 has to do with his Hebrew credentials. Moses claimed he wasn't the right person for the job and that the Hebrew community wouldn't receive him easily (an understandable concern after the rejection he experienced in chapter 2). Even Moses' insecurity over his speaking ability echoes the feelings of many who are raised without learning the language of their ethnic ancestors (and there's no biblical evidence that Moses had a speech impediment or stutter). Yet Moses' naming of his son in 2:22 seems to show that he hasn't completely adapted to Midianite life. See chapter 7 in *Invitation to Lead* by Paul Tokunaga for an excellent reflection on Moses' struggle here through an ethnic lens.

Question 4. Here are some examples: The author's attempts to work on his Spanish speaking reflect a desire to feel more like he belongs to his family's ethnic community. Often these steps involve picking up cultural markers or artifacts (language, clothing, foods).

Malcolm X writes about getting his hair straightened with lye in his *Autobiography*: "This was my first really big step toward self-degradation: when I endured all that pain, literally burning my flesh to have it look like a white man's hair. I had joined the multitude [who] . . . will even violate and mutilate their God-created bodies to try to look 'pretty' by white standards" (Alex Haley and Malcolm X, *The Autobiography of Malcolm X* [New York: Ballantine Books, 1999], 56-57).

The recent story of Rachel Dolezal could also be discussed. Born and raised in a white American family, she began identifying as Black in her twenties and became a college instructor, a leader in her local NAACP chapter, and a civil rights activist. When her ethnic ancestry became public, controversy about cultural appropriation and transracial identity swept the country.

Question 7. Moses might have killed the Egyptian because he wanted to change the situation of his people. He had enough of a sense of connection with the Hebrews to not only feel compassion but identify them as his people. To face the rejection that followed in 2:14 might have hurt him deeply, tipping him toward running away. Moses' resistance to God's call might have had roots in a sense that he wasn't "Hebrew enough" to lead these people.

Question 8. Here are some options Moses may have had: do nothing; speak to the Egyptian; gather other Egyptians to witness the abuse; petition Pharaoh to stop the abuse; practice nonviolent resistance, putting himself between the Egyptian and the Hebrew; join in the abuse; resolve to avoid Hebrews in the future; rally the Hebrews to revolt.

Question 9. Perhaps Moses thought he could spark a revolution. Or he might have not thought much beyond the moment. Perhaps he didn't feel he had the social capital to affect change any other way (according to Martin Luther King Jr., "A riot is the language of the unheard"). Moses might have thought that committing the murder was the only way he could make a break with his Egyptian upbringing and receive an embrace from the Hebrew community (Tokunaga, *Invitation to Lead*, 110).

Question 11. Some options are: God is gracious and generous; Moses had been prepared during his time as a shepherd; Moses needed healing and redemption; the Hebrews needed a leader with experience not being a slave; God has always intended salvation to come in partnership with humanity (through Abraham, Moses, Esther, Mary, and—ultimately—Jesus).

STUDY 4. NAVIGATING PRESSURE TO ASSIMILATE. DANIEL 1:1-21

PURPOSE: To challenge us to engage God in decisions about assimilation.

Question 1. They were carried off to Babylon together with articles from the temple (vv. 2-3); they were Israelite nobility (v. 3); they were handsome and smart (v. 4); they had no obvious physical conditions that would render them impure according to Hebrew religious standards (v. 4); they were already qualified to serve in the king's palace (v. 4); they did not know the language and literature of Babylon (v. 4); they were assigned food from the king's table (v. 5).

Question 2. They would have served as hostages to keep people back in Judea from revolting. The king might have wanted to offer an "uplift" narrative to his subjects: "Look at how good life could be under this new king." (For more on how these dynamics play out in history, see *Stamped from the Beginning* by Ibram X. Kendi and chapter six of Michelle Alexander's *The New Jim Crow*.) Perhaps the king just wanted the brightest and the best across the world to serve in his court. (A 2015 report by McKinsey & Company, *Diversity Matters*, makes a strong case that ethnic diversity provides a competitive advantage to organizations.)

Question 3. They're pressured to assimilate by learning the language and literature of the Babylonians (possibly including their "magic" and religious practices); changing their names; taking food and drink that would render them ceremonially unclean according to the religion of their community; and looking like all of the other young men who had been taken into the king's service.

Question 4. According to John H. Walton, Victor H. Matthews, and Mark W. Chavalas in *The IVP Bible Background Commentary: Old Testament*, "To change someone's name is to exercise authority over them and their destiny. . . . Since assimilation was ostensibly one of the objectives of the whole procedure in which Daniel was involved, a Babylonian name would be appropriate" (Downers Grove, IL: IVP Academic, 2000, 731). Each new name was related to a different Babylonian deity: Daniel ("God is my judge") is changed to Belteshazzar ("Bel protects his life"); Hananiah ("The Lord has been gracious") to Shadrach ("Command of Aku"); Mishael ("Who is what God is?") to Meshach ("Who is what Aku is?"); Azariah ("The Lord has helped") to Abednego ("Servant of Nebo"). Bel referred to Marduk, the primary god of the Babylonians. Aku was a moon god, and Nebo was a god of wisdom.

Question 6. Verse 8 tells us that Daniel resolved not to "defile" himself. Some think that Daniel and his friends didn't want to eat food that had been sacrificed to idols. Others think the issue had to do with Hebrew concern for ritual purity (see Leviticus). Still others believe that Daniel and his friends just picked an arbitrary line and said the assimilation had to stop somewhere. Good arguments exist for each view.

Question 9. In verse 2 God delivers the king of Judah and the temple over to the Babylonians. In verse 9 we see that God gave the chief official favor and compassion for Daniel (although the official still denied Daniel's request). In verse 17 God gives these young men knowledge and understanding of language and literature and gives Daniel the ability to interpret dreams. Your group might see other interventions by God not directly mentioned in the text.

Question 11. Orlando Crespo writes about the tension that comes with the need "to integrate into majority culture and also retain ethnic ways" (*Being Latino in Christ* [Downers Grove, IL: InterVarsity Press, 2003], 45). Be encouraged that this is more than a one-time decision, both for us and for Daniel and his friends.

STUDY 5. ETHNICITY AND THE GOSPEL OF CHRIST. EPHESIANS 2:1-22

PURPOSE: To lay a theological foundation for multiethnic community.

Questions 1 and 2. There are no wrong answers here. We just want to create space for the group to highlight particular portions of the passage that strike them, allowing the Holy Spirit to guide.

Question 3. Some possible answers are: we're saved from ourselves, our world, and the devil (vv. 1-3); salvation was necessary, but we couldn't save ourselves (vv. 1, 5, 8-9, 12); God saves us because he loves us (v. 4); salvation comes by grace (v. 5, 8); salvation removes our isolation and creates a new community (vv. 6, 13-16, 18-20, 22); God has a purpose for us in which salvation plays a part (vv. 7, 10, 15, 21-22).

Question 4. Jews might have resonated with Paul's language of transgressions and Jesus saving us despite our inability to keep the law. They might also struggle with the loss of privilege laid out in Paul's gospel of radical, multiethnic inclusion. Gentiles, on the other hand, might have picked up on the ethnic inclusion in a different way: Jesus includes the uncircumcised by faith, sets aside the ceremonial requirements of the law, and welcomes the Gentiles into the people of God—as Gentiles.

Question 5. Both Jews and Gentiles have full access to God through Christ. The ceremonial and ethnic requirements of the ancient Jewish law no longer serve as a barrier keeping Gentiles out (or requiring assimilation as an element of conversion). Everyone in Christ now experiences the full kindness of God. All are offered peace in Christ. Both Jews and Gentiles join God's family, uniting with the apostles and prophets to form God's new community.

Question 6. John Perkins shared this insight: "There is a gaping hole in our gospel. We have preached a gospel that leaves us believing we can be reconciled to God but not reconciled to our Christian brothers and sisters who don't look like us—brothers and sisters with whom we are, in fact, one blood. . . . Biblical reconciliation is *the removal of tension between parties and the restoration of loving relationship"* (*One Blood* [Chicago: Moody Publishers, 2018], 17).

Paul's explication of the gospel presents multiethnic community as a non-optional facet of the Christian life. In Christ, the people of God become a multiethnic people. No further option remains to stay divided. Reconciliation across ethnic lines is one of the products of Christ's finished work on the cross. People of every ethnicity stand on level ground at the foot of the cross. Ethnic heritage provides no ongoing advantage.

Question 8. Be aware that participants may have never engaged with ethnic reconciliation as an essential element of Paul's gospel narrative. This might be new to you too! Though we wish this wasn't the case, it presents a huge opportunity. We could see tremendous beauty as brothers and sisters in Christ connect across ethnic lines. As John Piper said on this topic: "Unity in diversity is more beautiful and more powerful than unity in uniformity" (*Bloodlines: Race, Cross, and the Christian* [Wheaton, IL: Crossway, 2011], 196).

Here are some tips to leading this conversation:

- Be patient with your group. You may have some who hesitate to elevate the conversation about ethnicity to "a gospel conversation." They're wise to move slowly. Let the Spirit and the Word do the heavy lifting.

- If this way of engaging the gospel is new to you, you have a chance to model openness, curiosity, and a posture of surrender to whatever the Bible teaches.

- Don't play the blame game. Many have heard teaching on Ephesians 2:8-9 without hearing about God's love (2:4) or his purposes for us (2:10). Given all of the historic challenges churches have had around ethnicity, it shouldn't surprise us that 2:11-22 has also often been set aside. Express gratitude for the people who have invested in you spiritually and honor that investment by continuing to grow.

- Paul's teaching in this passage shows up throughout his writing. This isn't an aberration. (See the "Now or Later" exercise at the end of this study.) Miss ethnic reconciliation, and you'll miss a core part of Paul's gospel presentation.

Question 10. One question that might come up at this point is whether the presence of ethnic-specific outreaches, ministries, or churches runs counter to the gospel picture in passages like this. This is a great question! Though a full answer remains beyond the scope of this study, here are some notes that might help.

The gospel makes it possible for every ethnic community to be reconciled to each other in Christ. In Christ, this is—in a mysterious way—our reality and our destiny. The history of ethnic segregation, injustice, and hierarchy in society has created conditions where the presence of some ethnic-specific outreaches, ministries, and churches remains necessary for the sake of safety, elevating marginalized voices, and engaging every corner of the world with the gospel.

Seek to understand the history of a ministry or church before criticizing it. Seek also to see its unique contribution to God's kingdom. The work of growing the ethnic diversity in a church is challenging, complex, and worth doing. For help in this, check out www.mosaix.info.

STUDY 6. UNITY THROUGH DIVERSITY. ACTS 6:1-7

PURPOSE: To grow in our ability to engage in multiethnic community in healthy ways.

Question 1. The conflict is ostensibly about the Hellenistic widows being ignored in the daily distribution of food. Commentaries disagree on whether these widows were just Greek-language speakers from the Jewish diaspora beyond Palestine or Jews who had assimilated to Greek culture. The church took care of widows but overlooked those from this ethnic community. In addition, the leaders of the church (the Twelve) all came from Hebraic backgrounds. Was the problem that they didn't care or that they didn't see?

Question 2. The ethnic thread of Luke's narrative in Acts is woven from the first page, when Jesus sends his followers to be witnesses to the ends of the earth. This passage in Acts 6 stands right before the start of a great persecution that led to the scattering of the church. The persecution started with the martyrdom of Stephen, one of the Hellenistic Jews appointed as a deacon. Justo Gonzalez makes the case that it is Hellenistic Jews, wishing to show their orthodoxy, who persecute the Christians (*Acts: The Gospel of the Spirit* [Maryknoll, NY: Orbis, 2001], 101).

Question 5. The Twelve could have ignored the complaint ("We answer to God, not these people"); shamed those who made the complaint ("Don't you remember how the people grumbled against Moses in the desert?"); responded with self-righteousness ("Don't you know how hard we work for the Lord?"); responded in anger ("How dare you criticize us!"); walked away ("If this is how you treat us, we'll take our ball and go home"); promoted segregation ("If you don't like it here, go start your own church"); or responded in shame ("Who are we to be leading? Jesus must have made a mistake!").

Question 6. Here are some examples: An anger response might have prevented future conflicts from coming to the surface, prohibiting the church from experiencing true community. An abandoning response might have led to the apostles missing out on a lifetime of meaningful service in, to, and through the church. A segregation response would have removed one of the most powerful aspects of the church's witness (as we saw in the previous study and at the end of this passage).

Question 9. Perhaps they believed that a group of Hellenistic Jews would have better access to the whole community and might be better positioned to make equitable distribution happen. Or they might have thought that this decision to give the Hellenistic Jews representation in the leadership of the church (albeit at a lower level in the hierarchy) would quiet the complaints. Maybe they also did this as a way of demonstrating repentance and making restitution (making them and their fellow Hebraic Jews vulnerable as a gesture of trust).

Question 10. Justo Gonzalez points out that "the apostles seek to keep for themselves 'the service of the word'; but the Spirit has other plans, and soon it is Stephen and Philip who are performing that ministry" (*Acts*, 94). We can possibly pick up a hint of immaturity in the Twelve, who resist "waiting tables" while proclaiming a Christ who washed feet. Their solution—apart from the Spirit's intervention—would have institutionalized an ethnic hierarchy in the church.

Question 11. Maybe the priests shared the benevolence responsibility and had a frontline perspective on how the church was making a difference in the city. Maybe the benevolence work of the church answered a concern for people on the outside that kept them from following Jesus: what will happen to our social institutions if we change? Maybe the people who received care from and felt seen by the church felt more comfortable being bold about their proclamation of their faith.

STUDY 7. ENGAGING ETHNIC TENSION. MATTHEW 15:21-28

PURPOSE: To connect what we're learning to Jesus and apply it to our lives.

Question 2. Without an ethnic identity, Jesus wouldn't be in touch with our struggles and frustrations around ethnicity (see Hebrews 4:15). We might believe that we had to abandon our ethnic identities in order to follow Christ and be united to him. He couldn't offer us healing, redemption, or relief from the pain and brokenness that has been handed down to us through the generations. We would each be tempted to treat him as if he were from our specific ethnic group, projecting our values onto him as a blank slate.

Question 4. Perhaps he didn't believe it was appropriate to heal her daughter. He might have been trying to teach his disciples a lesson about faith, inclusivity, prayer, or something else. He might have also wanted to make sure the disciples noted and were included in the conversation. Jesus could have been testing the woman to see why she was asking him for help or whether she really needed help. He might have been looking for a relationship that went deeper than a transactional miracle and hoping that his silence would create space for a more meaningful conversation. He might have perceived a complex cross-ethnic situation and felt his silence could invite the beginning of a candid connection.

Question 5. Some possible options are: you may not have standing to make the request; the person may not be able to fulfill the request; you may need to ask a few more times or in a few different ways; you might have offended the person you're asking; the person may be disinclined to acquiesce to your request; the person may not understand your request or why you need assistance.

Question 7. Ethnicity would have played a role in the conversation whether or not it was acknowledged directly, so Jesus just kept it in the open. Natalia Kohn Rivera writes, "He brought up race not to slap her with it but to surface it, to address it, and to redeem it" (Natalia Kohn Rivera, Noemi Vega Quiñones, and Kristy Garza Robinson, *Hermanas*

[Downers Grove, IL: InterVarsity Press, 2019], 112). Jesus honored both the woman's initiative and her worldview, observing her reference to him as "Son of David." Jesus wanted the woman, his disciples, and us to see something about the makeup of his kingdom: that Gentiles can be included, that they can be included as Gentiles (without converting to Judaism or adopting Jewish ethnic markers), and that persistent faith creates a new ground for inclusion in the people of God (replacing ethnic markers).

Question 11. They speak honestly with each other; persevere through difficult moments in the conversation; find common ground; exercise hope, faith, and compassion; listen closely to each other; use humor (Jesus' analogy and the woman's response contain some punning wordplay in the original languages); connect with the other without requiring the other to cease to participate in their own ethnic community.

Question 12. Jesus could have helped the woman without affirming her agency: "Fine, your daughter is healed." He also could have affirmed the woman's ability to influence the world around her without doing anything to actually help: "You have great faith. I guess you should keep praying, fasting, and hoping for the best." By offering the affirmation, Jesus shows the woman respect. By actually assisting, Jesus uses his privilege on the woman's behalf. His approach avoids paternalism and acknowledges the power differential in their relationship. In our experiences of ethnic tension, we might find opportunities to both acknowledge agency and actually assist. We might also find a need to ask others to do likewise for us.

STUDY 8. ETHNIC FOREVER. REVELATION 7:9-17

PURPOSE: To give us hope for our ethnic identities and our multiethnic communities.

Question 2. They are all wearing white robes and holding palm branches; they are all calling out in a loud voice in worship to the Lord; they have all suffered; they have the Lamb as their shepherd to lead them to flourishing; they receive God's comfort.

Question 3. Perhaps John picked up on phenotypic differences in hair, facial features, skin tone, and body type. Perhaps he heard multiple languages being spoken. Perhaps there were so many people that John knew no one ethnic community could account for all of them. Perhaps the Spirit gave John special insight into the origin of the crowd in order to, as Randy Woodley put it, "reject the myth of sameness" (*Living in Color* [Downers Grove, IL: InterVarsity Press, 2004], 34).

Question 4. There's no mention of distinctive clothing styles or foods. In fact, the whole crowd in the vision are wearing white robes.

Our past experiences of marginalization and ignorance shape how we tell our ethnic stories and, in some cases, whether or not we are even aware of our ethnic heritages. Our inclusion in this multiethnic community will change the way we see our ethnic selves and tell our ethnic stories.

The lived experiences of discrimination and abuse due to our ethnic heritages serve for many of us as boundary markers and bonding points for our ethnic identities. God's work to lead us to abundance and wipe away our tears will change our experience of our ethnic identities.

Question 5. While we don't know exactly how John knew of the full inclusion of every ethnic community, some distinctives must remain for him to make this claim.

The history of persecution, suffering, and tribulation experienced by this worshiping community is redeemed by God as he protects and provides in his kingdom. Some, if not much, of the pain acknowledged in this text will have been around ethnic identity and discrimination.

Question 6. Perhaps God wanted a full display of his creativity via the crowd. As John Perkins said, "We know just from looking at God's creation that he delights in diversity" (*One Blood*, 50). Perhaps God reveals himself through men and women created in his image, an image that would be complete only with a radical ethnic diversity (see Woodley, *Living in Color*). Perhaps God allows all kinds of people to remain the restored version of themselves in his presence. What if losing our ethnic identity would mean losing an essential part of ourselves? Perhaps God has ongoing, eternal purposes for humanity that require diversity.

Steve Tamayo is a strategist for InterVarsity Christian Fellowship, working in the Latino Fellowship and the Creative Labs. He has also served as the executive pastor at Chatham Community Church and the pastor of spiritual formation at Crossway Church. He lives in Tampa, Florida, with his wife and four children.